What Others Are Saying:

"If you look up 'alive' in the dictionary, you'll find Jennifer Hand's picture right there. If ever God created a woman full of passion and encouragement, He outdid Himself with Jenn. *25 Days of Coming Alive At Christmas* is full of that 'passion and encouragement!' Jenn has lived life on many levels and in many places, always telling the wonder of the story of Jesus as her sweetest message. Join her on this 25 day journey and be blessed by Jenn's loving heart this Christmas season!"

-- Jan Silvious, author of *Fool Proofing your Life, Same Life New Story,* International Speaker and Life Coach

"Has the story of Christmas become just another Bible story to you? As I opened the pages of *25 Days to Coming Alive at Christmas,* I realized that is what had happened to me. Each turn of the page, each day of the 25 day journey, ignited a fire in my heart, a renewed passion, for the magnificent glory found in the Christmas story. I unwrapped my Savior in a new way...a wonderful way. Join in this 25 Day Journey and come alive this Christmas!"

-- Wendy Blight, author of *Living So That* and *Hidden Joy in a Dark Corner,* Speaker and devotional writer with Proverbs 31 ministries www.wendyblight.com

"I have a sign in my kitchen that says this: 'Make time for the quiet moments, for God whispers and the world is loud' Amen right? I feel like the world gets even noisier around Christmas time. So many things view for my attention and it is easy for me to miss the whispers, the ones that remind me what is really important. I love Jenn's invitation to experience the Christmas story thought I am hearing it for the first time. What new things will I discover? What parts will blow me away? What have I been taking for granted l these years that He longs for me to fully know? This is the invitation she gives us, one that I will embrace fully this Christmas season because to know Him more fully means I am now able to make Him known more fully. And He is the perfect gift I can give anyone, any day of the year."

-- Jenn Ferguson, co-author of *Pure Eyes, Clean Heart: A Couple's Journey to Freedom from Pornography* and blogger at www.solideogloriasisterhood.com

25 DAYS TO COMING ALIVE AT CHRISTMAS

JENNIFER HAND

Acknowledgements

First of all, of course—Thankful to the Lord. He can call us to crazy things sometimes. Like **writing a 25 day devotional in a week!** Yes. You read that right. And God gave me the grace and the words, and I had the best time with Him in my cozy little writing corner on my couch. I am so thankful for the doors God opens, for the ways He is constantly doing more than we can imagine, and for His grace.

Granddaddy Alvin, this book is dedicated to you. It made my heart so happy how you read <u>31 Days to Coming Alive</u> and were so proud. So, I wrote this book for you. I miss you so much already, but I know you are having a blast in heaven. Thank you so much for always being full of life, fun, and love. I was so blessed to be your granddaughter.

Mom and Dad: You guys have given me so many incredible Christmas memories. I am the most incredibly blessed daughter in the world. (Well, Michelle is too, I guess!) I am so thankful for all you have taught me. I have especially learned how to laugh and hold on to hope in the darkest times with you. Michelle—my *wombmate*, well, you too have given me so many incredible Christmas memories. You are an amazing mama, wife to Todd and my best friend. I am so beyond blessed to have you as my one-minute-younger sister. Todd, you are an incredible brother—thanks for taking such good care of me. Alex, Hope and Abigail, being your aunt is the BEST job ever.

To my Coming Alive Board of Directors Family—I could not take this crazy journey without you. Thanks for all you do: Don and Debbie Sapp, Tresa Reeves, Diane Hundley, Shawna Hart, Michelle and Todd Humbert, Catrina and JP Pruitt, and Casey and Barry Lewis (our soon to be members!).

I cannot thank these two people enough for their contribution to this book. This crazy, last-minute God-sized dream would have never happened without Casey Bagley saying "yes" to edit my words. My victory sister, your editing on such a last minute to help people's lives be transformed by the truths in this book means so much more than I can express. You are a super talented blessed woman! And Ashley Wells, I could have never EVER done this without your gifted cover design and your formatting it so quickly to make into an e-book. What a gift you have my God-sized-dreaming friend. Check out Ashley's blog at www.ashleykwells.com

My Thursday night Bible study ladies: You make me come alive every week. I love our little community so much, and you have blessed me beyond words. Thanks for showing up every week and for being my bestest friends!

And lastly, my two pastors Chris Jessen and Jon Teague. You have taught me so much about Jesus this year. I cannot express what wonderful shepherds you are, and I am blessed to be one of your sheep. And Katie Jessen and Katie Teague: You ladies are incredible examples to me of anointed Proverbs 31 woman of God. You have impacted my life deeply. And my two heart sisters at church, Becca Calvert and Pamela Johnson: You girls have taught me how to listen well, how to love well, and how to live and laugh. Every time I leave your presence I feel closer to Jesus and more known by Him.

Table of Contents

Foreword.. 1

Coming Alive at Christmas 3

Day 1—God of the Details....................................... 9

Day 2—The Wait... 13

Day 3—Little is Much.. 17

Day 4—The Promise.. 23

Day 5—The Unexpected Fulfillment 27

Day 6—Light... 31

Day 7—Impossible Grace 35

Day 8—Impossible Tasks 39

Day 9—The Messy and the Broken.......................... 43

Day 10—Family Tree 47

Day 11—Watching 51

Day 12—The Exact Imprint..................................... 55

Day 13—The Halfway Point 59

Day 14—Wonderful Counselor 63

Day 15—Mighty God 67

Day 16—Everlasting Father...................................... 71

Day 17—Prince of Peace.. 75

Day 18—Following the Star...................................... 79

Day 19—The Cry of the Cross................................. 83

Day 20—O Christmas Tree 85

Day 21—Surprises from the Lord 89

Day 22—Childlike Wonder.. 93

Day 23—Jesus Presented at the Temple............................. 95

Day 24—We Lost Jesus... 99

Day 25—It's Christmas Day... 103

About Jenn... 107

About Coming Alive Ministries... 109

Foreword

The first time I ever met Jenn was at a Bible study she was leading that was meeting in my mom's living room. That evening, she reached into her Bible study bag to pull out her Bible and her lesson and instead pulled out....a pair of underwear! The look on her face was priceless!

I knew in that moment that God had placed a special kind of friend in my life. If only I had known then the beauty of the prayers she would pray over my life in the coming years, I may have been able to stifle the laughter that came rumbling out of my throat - a deep, side-splitting roar.

Jenn is my Victory Sister – my friend who holds me up to receive the promises of the Lord when my knees give way and my strength wanes. It is because of her faithful friendship that I am able to be a part of this devotional.

It is my prayer that your spirit can feel the steadfast love that Jenn has for the Lord and the genuineness that she wants you to experience Jesus in a renewed and refreshed way this Christmas.

Come alive with us as we celebrate the birth of the Son of God. Come alive knowing that the story of Christmas is a life-changing, heart-altering encounter with Emanuel, God with us!

Casey Bagley, Editor

Coming Alive at Christmas

Christmas is my favorite time of the year. True confession: I am one of those cheesy, love-all-the-traditions, get-the-joyful-butterflies-in-my-stomach, Christmas kind of girls. And I promise, you it's not all about gifts for me.

I am not saying I do not love a good gift or two, of course—I will accept any and all coffee cups and Starbucks gift cards.

I love the food, the family, the fun. I love the lights, the parties (oh, the Christmas party food—glory!), the music—the atmosphere of Christmas. And, of course, the Christmas story.

I wonder if you ever find the miracles of the Christmas story becoming normal to you. We have heard the story from beginning to end. Sometimes, before we realize what is happening, we can get caught in the trap of lumping THE Christmas story written in Matthew, Mark, Luke, and John with the Christmas spirit of a Hallmark movie's happily ever after.

The Christmas story is God's glory story. It is our redemption story. The cradle leads to the cross. The cross leads to our standing un-condemned.

It is this story that not only calls for celebration at the Christmas Eve candlelight service and the Christmas day reading from Luke Chapter 1, but also calls for us to come alive in celebration of Christ's birth every day.

I wanted to start the 25 days to Coming Alive at Christmas with this challenge to you (and me). Could you pretend as if you are hearing the miracle of the birth of Christ for the first time?

It is easy for the Christmas story to become normal. Mundane. The story we grow up hearing about. The story we sing along about in Christmas songs. The story we see in the nativity scene.

When I lived in Nepal as a missionary, it became un-normal for me. Each time I would tell someone about the Christmas story, I could see the wonderings and the questions in the eyes of those who had grown up worshipping idols.

God coming to earth as a baby? To take all our sins?

Emmanuel, God with us?

A virgin birth?

It was all new and all exciting to them.

I worry that for us good, Christian, church people it can become normal. Yes, God came to Earth as a baby. Yes, He was born to a virgin. *Silent Night, Holy Night, all is calm, all is bright*...now, let's get to the business, the hustle, the bustle.

I have a Christmas party to get to at church.

I want to share with you an actual blog entry from my first Christmas in Nepal in 2007.

Yes, 635 Christmas cookies, that is what I did yesterday. And before you get impressed, in pride I want to tell you, be *more* impressed. I made most of these cookies in the dark, with no electricity! (Wait, as I give myself a pat on the back and then repent for it!) Yesterday I was in the cookie making business. Knee deep in 5 kg of sugar (which you had to pick the bugs and dirt out of), mixing 2 tablespoons of milk, 2 tsp of baking powder, 1 cup sugar, 1/2 tsp vanilla, 1/2 tsp of salt, 1 3/4 cup flour, and don't forget the egg. I did a couple of times, but when you are making that many cookies, you use the batter anyway!

We made about 50 others besides the 635, but those were eaten by us, because you cannot give out a gingerbread man with an amputated arm or leg. You feel bad giving a Christmas tree cut in half, an angel with a broken wing (wasn't that a song once?), or a broken heart! So, if they broke, we ate.

Yesterday, for six hours, I baked cookies and listened to cheesy Christmas music. We made all these cookies for the Christmas play tomorrow. I am so excited about the play and ask for your prayers. This is the first big evangelical event they have done like this, and the people at the church took it seriously when I said invite non-Christians. In fact, so seriously that several people asked me tonight if they could come even if they were Christians.

So now, we have the cookies packed in cute little bags. The children have practiced how to *baa* like sheep. We have Mary, Joseph, a 2 year old Jesus (babies were hard to come by), a stable, and some really hilarious wise men. We are ready- just pray that God's light and truth SHINE!

It has been an incredible Christmas season. I have not bought one Christmas present or done any normal Christmas tradition, yet I am seeing the real reason for the season.

To share the glorious light of the gospel of Christ.

Would you like to know how that Christmas play turned out with me, a girl still learning to speak Nepalese and half of the time feeling I could not remember how to speak English, as the director? The baby Jesus (who was two) kept getting out of the manger. The goat that the shepherd had (hey, it was close enough to a sheep) ran away.

We had to start with the story of Adam and Eve since many of our Hindu neighbors had no context for the Christmas story. The "tree of good and evil" was a chili pepper plant in a pot. It had thorns. Eve got caught on the thorn and stuck. She had to exit the garden with the chili pepper plant stuck to her.

That crazy Christmas play changed my heart forever. The Christmas story came alive for me in a whole new way, through new eyes. That church was packed with those who had woken up that morning and placed flowers or offerings of food around their idols, hoping they could earn the favor of their gods.

Children wake up with wonder on Christmas morning, wondering what gift will be under their trees. Would you wake with wonder these 25 days? Each day will you ask God what gift He has wrapped in the story of Jesus coming to rescue you and me?

The Christmas story is the miracle of the God who created the heavens and the earth reaching out to me. To you. To offer us the greatest gift – a gift we get to open anytime, all the time, every time we are in need, even when we do not even realize we have a need.

I am excited for us to take time out of the busy and be blessed as we pause, wonder and come alive in the story of Christmas all over again.

Let's join with the angels in Luke Chapter 1:14.

"Glory to God in the highest, and on earth, peace among those with whom He is pleased".

Day 1—God of the Details

I hate the word "detail." I am a big picture kind of girl. I get excited about big vision. I always have a big idea or two running around my head, and I'm often praying for the miracle of the details to fall into place for the vision. I write To-Do lists and forget where I put them. Or, I end up forgetting the detail of buying coffee filters, so in the morning, when I desperately need my coffee, I may or may not use the To-Do list as a coffee filter.

I may or may not have gotten that from my Dad. He has been known to have as many as five businesses going in our house at once.

I remember a time as a child when we were trained to answer the "business" line at our house, which was actually the telephone in the extra bedroom.

Thank you for calling Hand Enterprises. Press 1 if you are interested in Victory Cues or in having a pool cue made. Press 2 if you need to speak to our representative about your computer needs. Press 3 if you want to speak to Mike about having professional billiard lessons. Press 4 if you would like to speak with a representative about Hand AV studios. Press 5 if you have forgotten all the options and have no idea why you are calling (and usually I would end up giggling in that process, as you can imagine).

This is only a SLIGHT exaggeration. My Dad is a big picture thinker—always excited about one thing or another, and so am I.

I am not great at details. I reluctantly started using a planner a few years ago. I use the term "using" loosely. You would know how reluctant I was if you knew that I picked the planner out, not based on its functionality, but based on the one I found the cutest and most inspiring to want to write in!

I may not be great at details, but I realize they are important. You need the details to fall into place if you want to see the vision accomplished. For that, you need detailed people. And, as I was meditating on the Christmas story this year, I was reminded how the Christmas story is a story of details. Little things that had to fall into place to make the BIG picture plan work out.

The big picture was a plan that was designed before the beginning of time to accomplish redemption and victory for the end of time. Now that is a BIG picture.

Part of the big picture of redemption through Jesus Christ involved a detail.

Micah 5:2 says, "But as for you Bethlehem, too little to be among the clans of Judah, from you One will go forth for me to be ruler in Israel. His goings forth are from long ago, from the days of eternity."

Detail: The Messiah to be born in Bethlehem.

The story of the details God worked out to make this happen can be found in Luke Chapter 2. Caesar Augustus had decreed a census which required you to travel back to your own town. (I am not sure a very pregnant Mary appreciated the detail of the long donkey ride home.)

This small detail of a census ushered in the fulfillment of prophecy from long ago. Joseph's home town was Bethlehem, just as the prophecy foretold.

The Christmas story is a story of God-driven, God-designed, God-woven details perfectly revealed in God's beautifully constructed ultimate plan of redemption.

Do you ever find yourself worried about all the details of your Christmas season? How will you get it all done, get it all bought, get it all finished?

Not just in the Christmas season, but in your life? How are the details going to work out for this financial situation, this family situation, this heartbreak in a relationship situation? It can be very easy for us to get caught up in trying to figure out details, finalize details, fit details into the story we believe we need to craft for our lives.

Come alive at Christmas today when you remember that the same God who detailed the Christmas story is detailing your life.

Rest in that. Trust in that. Lay your details at the feet of the One who knows the bigger story.

Christmas Heart Pause

Read Psalms 37:5. How does that impact you in light of trusting God with your details?

Read Ephesians 3:20. What are you looking for God to do that is abundantly above whatever you could ask, think, or imagine? Will you trust Him with the details?

Read Luke Chapter 2: 1-7, praising God for the way He used this census to fulfill His prophesied promised details. How has God used details that only He could have written into your story to fulfill His promise?

What details are you currently worried about, thinking about at night, wondering how they will work out? Take a moment to pray and commit those details to God.

Day 2—The Wait

Footie pajamas. I am going to let you in on a true confession. I have a grown up pair. Well, I do not know how grown up you can call these footie pj's. They have a giant sock monkey on them. Let's just say, when I wear them, I may or may not look like a giant, overgrown monkey myself. (Sorry, no pictures will be included.)

Footie pajamas make me think of kids on Christmas morning. Kids on Christmas morning make me think of words like *excited*, *eager*, *anticipation*. Take a moment and go back to your childhood, or think about your children now. The moments between eating turkey and watching the Macy's Day parade and the night your parents tuck you in on Christmas Eve felt like forever.

Then, there is the whole "you were expected to sleep" idea. How could you? Sleep just felt like another piece of the wait. The wait for Christmas morning. I remember my sister and I would try to make the waiting/sleeping thing more fun by putting every single doll and stuffed animal in our bed on Christmas Eve that we owned. I am not sure why we invited them to the party—but I guess we thought it would make the wait easier. What it really meant is that you would find me in the floor in the morning because those pesky dolls and animals took over the bed.

The pages of the Old Testament end in Malachi Chapter four. God has promised a Messiah, a rescuer, a redeemer, throughout the words of His prophets in the entire Old Testament. The Israelite people were familiar with their need for rescue, redemption, and the gift of freedom. Their whole history story had been one of release from bondage, a journey to a promise land, and then bondage again due to their slavery to sin.

My story can resemble their story at times. Jesus Christ has released me from bondage.

Galatians 5:1 says, "It is for freedom that Christ has set me free."

He releases me from the bondage of pride, approval addiction, and the fear that comes with these words. I experience the "promised land". Then, the next time I fear I disappointed someone, I slip back into the bondage of wanting everyone to love me, losing focus on the One who loves me with an everlasting love.

Galatians 5:1 also says, "Stand firm therefore, and do not be burdened again by a yoke of slavery."

Your bondage may look different from my bondage. Our sin struggles may change from day to day. But we are all in need of that freedom of the Savior - the Savior we can focus on as we celebrate the season of Christmas.

Do we anticipate the freedom and redemption God has written into our story with the same childlike wonder of the gifts on Christmas morning? *But as for you who fear my name, the sun of righteousness shall rise with healing in its wings. You shall go out leaping like calves from the stall.* (Malachi 4:2)

These words were proclaimed, and then there was silence. Four hundred years of silence, in fact, between the proclamations of Malachi and the pages of Matthew. After this very long pause, Matthew Chapter 1 bursts forth with the notes of hope found in the genealogy of Jesus Christ. The Messiah. The Rescuer. The One they had been waiting for.

All this took place to fulfill what the Lord had spoken by the prophet. Behold the virgin shall conceive and bear a son, and they shall call his name Immanuel (which means God with us). (Matthew 1:22)

The wait may have seemed long. But God never stopped working behind the scenes.

Even in the times when we may feel like God is not speaking, He is actively working behind the scenes.

We can live every morning with the anticipation of Christmas morning.

He is working miracles in your waiting.

Christmas Heart Pause

How have you seen God working behind the scenes in your story?

What freedom do you find yourself longing for? Re-read Galatians 5:1, and place your name and the sin you are struggling with in this verse. For example: *It is for freedom Christ has set Jenn free. Do not be burdened again by the burden of slavery to pride and longing for people's approval more than God's.*

Read Malachi 4. Pause and imagine those 400 years of silence. Then read Matthew 1 with the joyful hope of the end of waiting.

Day 3—Little is Much

You know the drill. You see the presents around the tree and you shake, rattle, and roll the package around to try to figure out what glorious thing is inside. My mom used to get very creative and put fun things inside the packages that would make noises as you shook the package.

It would seem at times, the bigger the package, the better the gift. I mean, truth be told, if you want to give me a new car to replace Toby the Taurus, you do not even have to wrap it. Just slap a bow on it and I will shout, "Glory!"

Sometimes, the best things come in little, tiny packages. Think about the excitement a new child brings into the family. That feeling of knowing things will never be the same with the birth of that little baby. When my nephew was born, I surprised my family by coming home for the birth. I had no idea how much love would burst in my heart as I held that little baby in my arms. He wrapped himself around my heart that day, and he still knows it. With his six-year-old, missing-a-few-teeth grin he often says, "Aunt Nenn, I know I can get anything out of you." He is right.

I believe we were created to long for more. To hope in the promised-yet-not-received. God has planted in us a longing for more so that we will look towards the hope of heaven. God's more for us often involves taking our little and doing much.

God's much is always more.

Mark 6:30 gives us an example of God taking little and doing much. Jesus and the disciples had been hanging out with a crowd of needy people. Jesus had been busy teaching them Truth. This was no small, intimate house gathering. This was a crowd of 5,000—and they were hungry. It was getting late, and the disciples were getting worried. Their logical situation would probably be the same as yours or mine. Send these folks home. They are hungry—the nearest McDonald's is too far away, and even if we ordered them all something off the dollar menu that would be more than our last gathering's love offering.

But Jesus was moved with compassion. I love that. *They were like sheep without a shepherd.* He told the disciples in verse 37, *"You give them something to eat."* Then, He asked the disciples what they had. What they had was very little. Five loaves and two fish.

Now, you may have grown up hearing this story so many times you forget to really get excited about the miracle that was to come. Jesus took that little and fed many. And there was more leftover.

When it is God taking the little and doing much, there is satisfaction and more leftover.

…and they all ate and were SATISFIED. And they took up twelve baskets full of broken pieces and of the fish. (Mark 6:42)

God intended to do much with the little package born in a dirty stable in Bethlehem.

God intends to do much with your little. Often we get so busy trying to be a lot, do a lot, and expecting a lot of how God should accomplish this thing or that thing, that we miss *His* thing.

Maybe you feel like you have little right now. You have little time to accomplish all the things you need to get done. You have little patience with your crazy two year old who makes a tornado look tame. You have little to offer to that friend. You have little faith that God will redeem that situation.

You have little resources and a big dream with lots of impossibilities.

You have little love for that family member. You have a big medical situation and the doctors have little answers.

The Christmas story is an example of God taking little and doing much.

In fact, the whole Bible is full of stories of God taking little and doing much—and His much is always more than we could have imagined on our own.

Think about some with me.

One little bunch of words—"Let there be…and there was..." (Genesis 1-2)

One little shepherd boy named David, one big giant. One little stone and much victory as the giant was slain. 1 Samuel 17

One little bit of flour, a little bit of oil and God provided a lot of provision for a widow. (1 Kings 17:8-16)

One little step and the Jordan River parted. (Joshua 3:15)

One little call from Jesus and a fisherman walked on water. One little finger of Jesus wrote in the dust and a woman caught in the sin of adultery was sent away uncondemned. One little band of disciples started one great big church. Jesus promised that one little mustard seed of faith would move mountains.

One little girl named Mary gave birth to one giant miracle. One little baby Jesus was born in a dirty stable and laid in a manger where animals ate.

One little drop of blood from this Jesus's nail pierced hands resulted in one big stone rolled away, one dead body brought to life, one resurrected Savior and much forgiveness of sins.

To God, little is much. Much is more. And more is enough to satisfy.

Christmas Heart Pause

Pick one of the stories listed above. Read through what God did through the seemingly little.

Where do you feel like you have *little* right now? Take that to God in prayer, opening your hands and heart, and ask God to take this little and do much.

Day 4—The Promise

Promise. The Webster definition of that word is "a declaration or assurance that one will do a particular thing or that a particular thing will happen." Generally, when we make a promise, we do intend to keep that promise. Sometimes, however, we make promises that we know we will not be able to keep. Still other times, we find ourselves breaking the promise unintentionally. And, in the good times, we keep the promises we make.

I promise myself every Monday that I am going to eat healthy that week. *True confession: I often break that promise by Monday night.*

I promise myself I am going to get more organized. *True confession: I need a full-time assistant for that.*

I will keep your deep secrets of the heart. You can trust me in that. But, if you tell me something exciting that you want to keep a surprise, I cannot promise that I will be the best keeper of your secret.

I cannot help it. I just get so excited about things. Like if a friend tells me she is pregnant. Or if there is a surprise party. I cannot promise you that I will not accidently giggle, grin, and let the secret out.

Our God is a promise-keeper. And truth be told, like me, He is not always the best at keeping exciting-news types of secrets. He did not keep the promise of a Messiah to come a secret. In fact, He wanted to make sure to proclaim the promise. He proclaimed the promise so people would hold on to hope and expectation and feel an eagerness to meet the Messiah.

I imagine the excitement God had about this promise. About the fulfillment of this promise. The promise of hope for the hopeless, freedom for the captive, and salvation from a Savior.

Behold the virgin will conceive and bear a Son and shall call his name Immanuel. (Isaiah 7:14)

For to us a Child is born, to us a Son is given; and the government shall be upon his shoulder and his name shall be called Wonderful Counselor, Mighty God, Everlasting Father, Prince of Peace. Of the increase of his government and of peace there will be no end, on the throne of David and over His kingdom. (Isaiah 9:6-7)

I love the feeling that comes when you fulfill a promise. I promised my nephew a donut date last week, and I loved the joy of fulfilling that promise. I love watching him enjoy and experience the fulfillment of that promise.

I cannot begin to imagine the atmosphere in heaven the day Jesus was born as a fulfillment of a promise made from the beginning of time. Take a moment. Pause. Close your eyes, and imagine you were there. It's no wonder the angels came singing, "Glory to God." I would be doing some glory shouting myself. In fact, I almost just let one slip out as I typed this in this coffee shop.

24

You were on His mind when He fulfilled that promise. He wanted a relationship with you. He no longer wanted you to have to go through priests and animal sacrifices. He wanted to provide Himself as the sacrifice.

Therefore brothers, since we have confidence to enter the holy places by the blood of Jesus, by the new and living way that he opened for us through the curtain, that is through his flesh and we have a great high priest over the house of God, let us then draw near with hearts in full assurance of faith. (Hebrews 10:19)

The hope of Christmas is in a Savior who keeps His promises.

…of this man's offspring God has brought to Israel a Savior, Jesus, as he promised. (Acts 13:23)

As. He. Promised.

You and I may not be faithful to keeping our promises, but our God is. And He has made so many powerful promises. His final promises are found in Revelation, and they involve victory. His in-between promises are found throughout the pages of His living Word.

And the story we are living out is in between the pages of Jude and Revelation.

Wrap yourself in the warm blanket of truth today that God will keep His promises to you.

Christmas Heart Pause

What is a promise found in the pages of God's word that you have experienced God keep for you? Take a moment and thank God for keeping those promises to you.

What promise of scripture do you need for your situation today? Write out a few verses somewhere. Index cards, on your bathroom mirror, on your hand.

Let us hold fast the confession of our hope without wavering for he who promised is faithful. (Hebrews 10:23)

Day 5—The Unexpected Fulfillment

I wish you and I could be chatting together. I just moved to a coffee shop to write and am sipping on a sinfully good white chocolate raspberry latte. I can drink anything from strong black coffee to feels-like- you-are-sipping-dessert coffee. Today is a dessert coffee kind of day. So let's pretend to have coffee together.

Yesterday we talked about promises.

We were reminded that our God is a promise-keeper. However, many people in the time of Jesus missed the good news that the birth of Jesus was the fulfillment of their promised Messiah. They were looking for a certain kind of Savior. They were looking for the fulfillment of the promise to play out in a certain way according to their certain plan. They were expecting a political Messiah, a battle-conquering hero type.

Many missed the promised Messiah because the promise did not come in the plan, package, or place they expected.

For my thoughts are not your thoughts, neither are your ways my ways, declares the Lord. For as the heavens are higher than the earth, so are my ways higher than your ways, and my thoughts than your thoughts. (Isaiah 55:8-9)

I can find myself making really big plans and expectations. Having thoughts of the way a situation should turn out. How a story should go. A ten year plan for tomorrow.

I wanted to be a doctor. I was going to be a doctor until I took Biology 101 in college. And then I quickly changed my major to church vocations. I could not imagine doing surgery on a real person as much as my hand shook dissecting that frog. And let's not mention how I confused the heart for the stomach. You can breathe a sigh of relief that God's thoughts were higher than mine.

I think about who I would have married if my eighth grade thoughts and plans had come to fruition. I think about what I would have missed if I had let my small thoughts drive God's big plans. Pausing to think about this makes me want to shout glory for God's higher ways. But it also makes me wonder how often I have missed seeing the fulfillment of God's promise to me because it did not come in the plan, package, or place I expected.

From the beginning, the enemy has planted lies that our God's plans are not enough. He whispered in Eve's ear that surely, if she ate of the tree God told her not to, she would be like God.

Have you ever watched a two year old throw a temper tantrum? You know the throw-yourself-down-on-the-ground, kick-and-scream-and-make-a-scene type? I wonder if you have ever want to throw an adult temper tantrum yourself.

Things do not seem to be going your way. The plans you have are falling through. The job is not meeting your expectations. Your friend secretly unfriended you on social media. Your house never looks like the ones on the Mommy blog. Your holiday plans are not feeling so fa-la-la. You begin to wonder if God is a fulfiller of promise. Can what He says in Jeremiah 29:11, "For I know the plans I have for you, declares the Lord, plans for wholeness and not for evil, to give you a future and a hope," be true?

The hope of a Messiah was fulfilled in the package of a little baby. Born to a girl that had no idea she would be the mother of the Messiah until an angel showed up in her room.

This baby was born in a stable, because even the Motel 6 was full. How could a Messiah be born this way? God keeps His promises.

He is keeping His promise to you. Even when the fulfillment is unexpected. It may be Him granting you peace in the process. It may be Him walking you through the fire and you not getting burned. It may be Him removing a relationship completely from your life. It may be Him providing in the last minute in the way you least expect.

He is fulfilling His promise to you.

Christmas Heart Pause

Read Ephesians 3:20. How have you seen God fulfill His more-than-you-could-ask-or-imagine promise to you?

29

Read Luke Chapter 2:1-21. If you could have imagined the coming of a Messiah, how would you have imagined the fulfillment of the promise? Why do you think God planned the story this way?

Celebrate with Jesus the moment when He opened your eyes to not miss the promise of a Savior.

Day 6—Light

I appreciate the gift of light. I spent two winters in Nepal where they had this dreadful thing called "load shedding." This meant that you were on a power schedule and were given a certain amount of power each day. As the winter progressed, the amount of power decreased. Some days, we would have two hours of power, and often that scheduled time would be in the middle of the night.

Doing everything by candlelight became the new normal of our lives. If you are a handsome fellow and want to take me on a romantic dinner out, let's skip the candlelight. After living by candlelight for two years, I like light so much that I would not mind to eat under the brightest fluorescent light possible.

And, if you know me, you know I do not have the best track record with candles. I tend to accidently light things on fire *more times than I can count*. I have not burned down my house yet, but I have burned down an outhouse, caught my friend's hair on fire at a candlelight service, and caught a backdrop on fire while speaking, all at different times.

Ann Vonskamp says this in her book *The Greatest Gift*: "When you light a world and the unexpected places with a brave flame of joy; when you warm the cold hopeless places with the daring joy that God is with us, is for us,

God is in us, then you are a wick to light hope in the dark."

God's light was meant to break into our darkness. The miracle of Christmas is the light flung from heaven to earth.

Emmanuel—God with us.

The people who walked in darkness have seen a great light; those who dwelt in a land of deep darkness, on them has light shined. (Isaiah 9:2)

I am praying for you. I am praying that if you are in the midst of circumstances that feel like darkness, you will experience a reminder of God's light.

No matter how deep the darkness, light can always break through. Hold on my friend, hold on.

If you are in a season of light, I am praying you will spread the light.

In Luke 1:67, John the Baptist's father, Zechariah, was filled with the Spirit and began to prophesy about Jesus. I love verses 78-79 in the Message version, which is a paraphrase of the Bible.

Through the heartfelt mercies of our God, God's Sunrise will break in upon us. Shining on those in the darkness, those siting in the shadow of death, then showing us the way, one foot at a time, down the path of peace. (Luke 1:78-79)

I used to take my campers caving at the summer camp that I worked at. Secretly, I despised caving. I did not like the closed in feeling of the cave walls. I did not like the tight spaces. I really did not like the darkness. Once we would crawl through the mud and tight spaces deep inside the cave, we would have all of the campers turn their headlamps off. Caves are the only place in the world where there is absolute darkness. I always had a fear that all of the headlights would malfunction, and we would never see light again.

We would talk about Christ being the light. How we can bear His light. And then, after seemingly an eternity sitting in the darkest of the dark, we would have one camper turn on his light. When that light turned on, we would all breathe a collective sigh of relief. That one light pierced through the darkness.

Jesus Christ pierced through the darkness and His nail-pierced hands are always welcoming us into His light.

God is light and in him there is no darkness at all. If we walk in the light as he is in the light, we have fellowship with one another, and the blood of Jesus his Son cleanses us from all sin. (1 John 1:5,7)

Christmas Heart Pause

Find some Christmas lights. Turn off the room lights, and notice the effect the Christmas lights have on the room. Spend some time thanking Jesus for the way His light pierced the darkness.

Who is someone you can share the light of Jesus with? Spend some time praying for them.

Read 1 John 1:5-10 about walking in the light.

Day 7—Impossible Grace

I just feel like we are friends here. And I thought you might want in on something that literally just happened. I was pulled over at Sonic. It was happy hour, and I wanted a Diet Coke with extra lime. Apparently, so did the cop that came to the stall next to me. I knew I was in trouble when he turned on his blue lights and pointed at me.

Who gets pulled over at a drive-in fast food restaurant stall? *Me.*

My car, Toby the Taurus, has quite the personality. One of those being his "Check Engine" light will not go off. Even after hundreds of dollars of work. That bright orange engine light is still on. Where I live, you have to pass a car emissions test to renew your registration. It is always like going to the car principal's office for me. I drive into the "office" and usually end up leaving grounded. Since I cannot pass the engine class, Toby's tags…expired. Expired tags equals getting pulled over at Sonic—if you are me.

So now, I am praying for the impossible. For that light to go off and for Toby to pass emissions so I don't have to pay a ticket. This is a small "impossible" I am praying for. Last year, in a hospital waiting room, we were told my father would not live through the night. I prayed the big "impossible." I prayed for God to heal him. And He did.

Our God is a God of the impossible. The Christmas story is packed full of the impossible.

A virgin Mary with child. A fiancé named Joseph who agrees to take Mary as his wife, risking his reputation. Angels appearing to shepherds in a field by night. A star guiding several wisemen to the place where Jesus lay.

The most impossible? The God of the universe came. He came into the earth in the form of a tiny baby boy, so He could take the magnitude and weight of sin onto His shoulders. He left the glory of heaven to walk the dusty streets of Earth.

In the beginning was the Word, and Word was with God, and the Word was God. He was in the beginning with God. All things were made through him, and without him was not anything made that was made. (John 1:1-3)

Let's go back to the beginning. Genesis. Genesis tells the story of a God who creates something out of nothing. He does this by spoken word. He said, "Let there be," and there was.

...and the Word became flesh and dwelt among us, and we have seen His glory, glory as of the only Son from the Father, full of grace and truth. (John 1:14)

And from His fullness we have all received grace upon grace. (John 1:16)

The word became flesh. The word became flesh to gift us with grace. I love how John states it as "grace upon grace." Not just a little bit of grace. A lavish amount of grace. Grace full of impossible mercy.

My incident with the cop today reminded me of a time I was granted mercy. I was the cause of an accident. Not only was I the cause of an accident, but I had left my purse with my driver's license in my boss's car that night. And my tags were expired (same problem with emissions passing). When the police officer came to my window the first words out of my mouth were, "That was my fault."

I do not think he was expecting that. My admission of guilt seemed to cause him to want to grant me mercy, which I did not deserve. He did not write me a ticket for any of my offenses. He let me go, even in the admission of my guilt. (And I practically wanted to kiss his feet for it!)

For all have sinned and fallen short of the glory of God and are justified by grace as a gift through the redemption that is in Christ Jesus. (Romans 3:23)

…because if you confess with your mouth that Jesus is Lord and believe in your heart that God raised him from the dead, then you will be saved. (Romans 10:9)

In confessing our guilt we get the gift of God's grace. What a glorious gift!

Would you take a moment in the hustle and bustle of the Christmas chaos to let the gift of God's grace wash over your soul?

God's impossible grace was made possible through Jesus. Jesus made the impossible possible by ushering the kingdom of heaven to Earth. He was born, and thirty plus years later, He was crucified on a cross for our sins. Three days later, He rose again.

Heaven came to Earth then returned back to heaven.

The impossible made possible.

Christmas Pause Response

How have you experience God's grace this week? Thank God for the gift of grace.

Read John 1:1-19. Which part speaks most to your heart? Celebrate the Word becoming flesh and dwelling among us.

Day 8—Impossible Tasks

Yesterday, we bathed ourselves in the impossible gift of grace made possible by the sacrifice of Jesus. Whew. It still takes my breath away a bit when I think about the love God has for me—and for you. John 3:16 style.

For God so loved (put your name in it) that He gave his only God, that whoever believes in Him shall not perish but have eternal life.

His love sent His son into your world. To rescue you from your sin. Today, we are going to visit the Earthly mother of this miracle One. Her name is Mary. We find her in the midst of her ordinary story. Her story quickly moved from ordinary to extraordinary the minute an angel visited her room.

This was not just any angel either. It was the angel Gabriel. The first words out of His mouth were in Luke 1:28, "Greetings, O favored one, the Lord is with you." It says that she was "greatly troubled" at these words and wondered what this greeting meant.

I think I would be more than a little troubled if a giant of an angel named Gabriel showed up in my room on an ordinary day. Or any day, really. Visitations from angelic beings are hard to come by. My last apartment had a lady named Zelda that lived above me. If I did not answer the door and she knew I was home, she would just march on in. Once, I came out of the shower to find her sitting in my living room. I screamed fairly loudly, and Zelda was not an angel.

The angel's next statement showed He was not surprised by Mary's distress. He told her not to be afraid.

...and the angel said to her, "Do not be afraid, Mary, for you have found favor with God. And behold, you will conceive in your womb and bear and son, and you shall call His name Jesus. He will be great and will be called the son of the Most High. And the Lord God will give to Him the throne of his father David, and He will reign over the house of Jacob forever and of His kingdom there will be no end." (Luke 1:30-33)

Have you ever had that moment when you received news, good or bad, that just shocked the socks right off of you? Or the flip flops, if you are me. (It was 20 degrees outside today, and I went out for coffee in my flip flops. Crazy, I know!) That news that you were not expecting. You have been promoted. You have been demoted. You find out that guy really does like you. You find out that girl really does not like you at all.

You get news of medical tests that you were not expecting. You get news of healing from a medical condition that you were not expecting. You get asked to take a leadership position in church, and you wonder if they meant to say your name. You are called by God to be a stay-at-home mom, or to homeschool your children. You are called by God to send your children to school. You are a student completely overwhelmed by the school work at hand. You are a pastor shepherding a bunch of lost sheep. You are a college student, and God asks you to change your major. You are graduating from college, and you have no idea what steps are next. You are called by God to write a devotional for 25 days to Coming Alive at Christmas in one week. (Raising my hand on that one!)

We find ourselves in situations that seem impossible. Tasks that God has prepared in advance for us that we cannot possibly imagine pulling off. Miracles that you are not sure will be accomplished.

Imagine being called to be the one who changes the diapers of Jesus, the son of God. There were not enough mommy blogs with their great ideas to even begin to help Mary feel qualified for this motherhood calling.

Imagine worrying about your reputation and how you would explain, not just to your finance, but to the world— that the baby inside of you was conceived by the Holy Spirit. That this baby that you are carrying was the Son of God. No gender reveal party needed when an angel announces your baby's birth.

This is the part that stuns me about Mary. What is her response in the light of the impossible? She accepts the impossible, therefore allowing God to do the work to make it possible.

And Mary said, "Behold, I am the servant of the Lord, let it be to me according to your word." (Luke 1:38)

Can you insert those words into your situation? Can you offer back what seems impossible to the God that makes anything possible?

Behold, I am the servant of the Lord is this situation. Even when it feels scary. Beyond my resources. Beyond my ability. Impossible really.

I am the servant of the Lord.

Christmas Heart Pause

What "impossible" do you hear God calling you to this season? Talk to the Lord about the fears. Then hear Him whisper, like the angel Gabriel, "Do not be afraid."

Read Luke 1:37.

Pick your favorite story in the Bible of God doing the impossible. Read that story as encouragement to your heart.

Day 9—The Messy and the Broken

My sister and I amused ourselves with our big imaginations in hilarious ways as children. It is so much fun to be an identical twin—you always have a playmate to get into mischief with. Actually, I was often the one convincing my sister into the mischief, and she was a saint and would usually take the blame for it.

We had this thing about pretending we were on a mixture of a home décor and a do-it yourself craft show. This was before the days of HGTV and TLC. I bet you wished you could have tuned in. Two identical, blonde-haired, blue eyed twins, often dressed alike, teaching you how to make things we really had no idea how to make.

Christmas was one of our favorite times to play this game. Let's just call our show "The Handy Twins." The Handy Twins loved to use the Christmas tree as our object lesson and pretend to tell you, not only how to decorate the tree, but how to make the ornaments on the tree. One year, for some strange reason, I had this crazy issue with the Christmas tree. Every time I went by the Christmas tree, before I knew what was happening, the Christmas tree would start to teeter to one side. Then, quick as lightning, that Christmas tree would fall over—on top of me. Repeatedly, the other half of Handy Twins, my sister Michelle, would have to unbury me from beneath the evergreen fake Christmas tree. I am not sure how one "professionally" recovers from that sort of incident on their "DIY décor show," but I usually recovered by calling a commercial break for our pretend audience.

We lost a few ornaments that year in the mess of the Christmas tree falling over. Our Handy Twins Christmas show also provided some other casualties for a bright, shiny group of ornaments.

I could not help it. I like shiny things. And these particular ornaments glistened with a brilliant crystal pattern of color. And so they were the ones I would pretend to teach how to make on our pretend TV show. I would get excited. I would talk with my hands. I would show the beautiful colors, the reflection the light made on the glass. And then it would happen. I would stick my finger up close to the crystal, very-breakable center, and – oops, my finger would slip—and it would break in the middle. Broken. Every time.

Of course I did not want my mom to know that I had broken her ornament, so the first one I broke I hid under the television cabinet, swearing my sister to secrecy. Then, came ornament break number two. Then three. Then four. Then five. Soon, there were the remains of a broken, messy Christmas hidden away, and the shiny, bright crystal ornaments were no longer hanging for all to see.

Do you ever try to hide your brokenness, sweeping it into a closed room in your heart thinking no one will notice the shiny parts are gone? Like the tree falling over, sometimes life circumstances fall, and we find ourselves noticing a mess in the aftermath. When you recover from the impact, you notice, as you put things back together, it never quite looks like it did before.

Things start to fall apart in your marriage or relationship.

A friendship gets messy when you least expect it.

Your church has a split. Your school financial aid falls through. Your teenager runs away. Your ministry is not getting the response you were praying for.

Like the shiny ornaments, sometimes we create the brokenness with our own hands. We make mistakes that cause our relationship to fall apart. A sin struggle that causes consequences. We find ourselves hanging onto hurts so long that bitterness keeps our heart from being free.

It can be so easy to want to pretend when things get broken and messy. To sweep the broken pieces and pretend things are not messy.

The problem is, eventually this brokenness will find us out. Eventually, someone will notice the shine is gone off the tree. That something is missing. Or they will find the broken pieces.

My mom found the broken ornaments I had hidden. I am pretty sure I got a good-sized talking to about hiding things and was told not to walk near the Christmas tree again. We kept those ornaments and still hang what is left of them on the tree every year as a family joke. I see it more as a reminder. A reminder that we do not have to hide our broken things.

The Spirit of the Lord is upon me, because He has anointed me to proclaim good news to the poor. He has sent me to proclaim liberty to the captives and recovering of sight to the blind, to set at liberty those who are oppressed, to proclaim the year of the Lord's favor. (Luke 1:18-19)

Jesus came into the broken world - came to redeem our brokenness, not sweep it under the rug.

He came to set us free. Even at our messiest. *Especially* at our messiest.

And when life circumstances or our own decisions create chaos and mess, He still can make us sparkle when we reflect His light from our broken pieces.

Christmas Heart Pause

Read 2 Corinthians 3:17-20. In light of this verse, ask God to reveal any broken parts you may have tried to hide and transform those pieces into His glory.

Continue reading in 2 Corinthians 4:5-6. How can God's light reflect off what may have felt like darkness for you?

Day 10—Family Tree

Once I decided not to keep my major as pre-med and become a famous surgeon (can we wall say amen?!), I majored in human services and church vocations. In our human services classes, we did studies on the concept of genograms. This is a fancy term for looking at your family tree. Going back and noticing relationships, patterns and people that make up your family of origin.

One of our assignments was to make a giant poster-sized version of our family tree on both sides. Of course, my sister and I had the project finished almost as soon as our wonderful (and I must say my favorite teacher) asked. Ok, that is a boldfaced lie. We waited, as usual, until the last minute.

I remember us both huddled over our poster pages in the lobby of dorm, working into the wee hours of the morning to map our family on this tree. My family gets a bit confusing with some of the cousins on my Dad's side. Several have been married many times and have a bunch of kids. Truth be told, I have a hard time remembering who is who and keeping up. So I may or may not have fudged some on our family tree on that side. My sister may or may not have done the same.

But we did not tell each other we could not remember our second cousins third wife. Or the other names we could not remember. We probably should have collaborated. I realized that a bit late when the teacher asked us after we turned in the project how identical twins could have different names on their family tree!

Family names and family lines were very important in the Bible. There are chapters in the Bible that I bet you have skipped over because you did not want to read that long list of names (1 Chronicles anyone?).

Matthew 1 opens with the genealogy of Jesus Christ. You may think you need an extra shot of espresso to get excited about the names listed in Matthew 1:1-17. And you pray you never have to be the one to volunteer to read that passage in Bible study and have to pronounce *those* names.

I hate it when I volunteer to read a passage of scripture and realize those names are the ones I am going to have to pronounce. Shealtiel and Zerubbabel anyone?

These names in Matthew 1 do, however, call for excitement. They represent that God is a promise keeper.

God said, "No, but Sarah your wife shall bear you a son, and you shall call his name Isaac. I will establish my covenant with him as an everlasting covenant for his offspring after him." (Genesis 17:19)

Matthew 1 opens with Abraham as the father of Isaac, Isaac the father of Jacob, and then the story continues. God's faithfulness to His covenant with Abraham, an everlasting covenant for his offspring after him.

And your house and your kingdom shall be made sure forever before me. Your throne shall be established forever. (2 Samuel 7:16)

God was making a promise to David that He would establish His kingdom through David—a kingdom that would be established forever.

Fulfillment of this promise. Jesus. In the genealogy of Jesus, we find David listed in Matthew 1:5 and 6.

The names in Matthew 1 also represent that God uses the imperfect, the inconsistent, and the unexpected to accomplish His will.

Rahab. She was a prostitute. Her name made the Jesus family tree.

Ruth. She was an outsider. A foreigner who did not belong to the Israelite people. Her name made the Jesus family tree.

David. He committed adultery and then murdered the husband of the one he committed adultery with.

His name made the Jesus family tree.

This makes those names so much more exciting! God knows we are imperfect. He knows we are inconsistent.

Our name can make the Jesus family tree.

Christmas Heart Pause

Draw a simple picture of your family tree. What is your family's story?

49

Draw a simple picture of Jesus' family tree from Matthew 1. (No need to get elaborate folks. There will be NO grade. Just consider yourself getting an A plus right now.) Then, put your name on that tree.

Celebrate: Your name made the Jesus family tree!

Day 11—Watching

I was an angel in a live nativity scene once. I wondered at the time if strapping the angel wings on me attached to a white choir robe would transform me into an angel. The truth is, the wings made no difference at all. Neither did the halo. Especially at the moment when the donkey beside me started eating my wings.

I kept getting the stop moving look from the director of the live nativity scene. But it is hard to stop moving when your wings are being chomped on by a donkey. And in case you did not know, donkeys have very BAD breath.

It's hard to keep your halo on straight while balancing your being-chewed-on wings and standing with your arms outstretched like a good angel stands. In fact, it is hard to keep your halo on at all. I finally succumbed to that little giggle that I felt inside. And once that one giggle came out—many more followed. Suddenly, the atmosphere of the live nativity changed drastically when the angel doubled over laughing.

Let's just say, I was never given the position of angel again.

...and in the same region there were shepherds out in the field, keeping watch over their flock by night. And an angel of the Lord appeared to them, and the glory of the Lord shone around them, and they were filled with fear. (Luke 1:8)

Have you stopped to think of the significance of God sending the angels to a bunch of stinky shepherds in the night? Ever wondered why God found this so significant that He wrote it in the pages of Luke right after chapter 2 verse 7 tells of Jesus being laid in a manger?

I love that God chose stinky shepherds to be the first to announce His birth. This was pre-social media days. If Jesus was born today, maybe there would be a #messiahborn that would trend on Twitter. God could have gone to the palace, to the princes, to those in powerful positions. Instead, He went to the shepherds.

Shepherds had a rough life. They faced dangers from wild animals and thieves alike. They endured the elements of outside. They had to stick it out in storms and stay on alert constantly, all to protect their sheep.

The position of a shepherd required great watchfulness, especially in the darkness of night. God chose to reveal the secret of His son to those who would be watching even in the darkness.

And the angel said to them, "Fear not, for behold, I bring you good news of a great joy that will be for all the people. For unto you is born this day in the City of David, a Savior, who is Christ the Lord. And this will be a sign for you; you will find a baby wrapped in swaddling cloths and lying in a manger. And suddenly there was with the angel a multitude of the heavenly host praising God and saying, "Glory to God in the highest, and on earth peace among those with whom he is pleased!" (Luke 2:10-14)

I love how personal the angels made it. They made sure that the shepherds knew this was the story of their salvation. Not just for the king in the palace, but for the shepherd in the pasture.

Unto. You.

Friends, unto you is born a Savior which is Christ the Lord.

I want to be watchful like the shepherds. The secrets of the Son were revealed to them as they watched.

What if this Christmas we watch? Watch for the Lord in our stories? Watch for the ways God is revealing His glory? Watch for Jesus in the cashier in the checkout line? Watch for Jesus in the time with our family? Watch for Jesus by studying His words? Watch for Jesus by listening to His voice?

Watchful and worshipful. Those stinky shepherds wasted no time. As soon as the angel left proclaiming this good news, they went to where the good news was.

They made haste.

They made haste and found Jesus.

Let's watch. Let's wait. Let's listen. And as we watch, let's find Jesus. In our hours, in our minutes, in our days.

When we find Him, like the shepherds, let's worship him. Let's be filled in wonder about Him.

Christmas Heart Pause

Are you watching for the secrets of Jesus to be revealed to you? Ask Him to meet you like He met the shepherds. What do you sense Him speaking to your heart?

How have you seen God reveal His glory this week?

The angels burst out in song. Write down your favorite song of praise, sing your favorite song of praise. Just take a moment and burst out into song with the angels.

Day 12—The Exact Imprint

I am an identical twin. What a fun joy that has been! People ask me all the time what it is like. I thought I would take the time here in this space to answer that question. *I am not really sure what it is like to be an identical twin.* Why? I have always been an identical twin; I have never experienced the opposite.

I love being born with my best friend. Sometimes I still call her my *womb mate*. I have always loved that I was born first. One minute to be exact. That one minute made me the oldest, and I made sure she knew it. I talked her into the craziest schemes by saying, "But I am the oldest." I feel true confessions are good for the soul, so let me tell you one of the schemes I still feel bad about.

It was third grade reading class. I sat in the chair in front of her. I had been feeling lazy and did not do my reading homework, and she did. She had a perfect paper, and I had one that was going to receive a zero. I passed her a note and my undone homework and convinced my saint of a sister to put my name on her paper and her name on mine. Her paper now a zero, mine an A plus. The story gets worse. The teacher said her paper needed to be signed by a parent, so I convinced her to forge my mom's signature. Keep in mind, we had just learned to write in cursive. The "V" was a hard one to get down, and the teacher immediately recognized that it was not my mom's handwriting. So, she had my sister write sentences stating that she would not forge her parent's signature. Those were supposed to be signed.

I convinced her that I had practice the cursive "V" in Vicky and that the teacher would surely not suspect. So again, she signed my mom's name. The teacher figured it out quickly—and called my parents to let them know what Michelle had been doing. Michelle got in BIG trouble, and I did not. She did not tell them that this whole plan was my fault.

Whew, I feel better after confessing my third grade sins to you.

We are the exact DNA imprint of each other, but we can be very different.

Jesus was the exact DNA of God the Father. I must admit, there are times I simply cannot wrap my mind around the Trinity. God the Father, the Son, and the Holy Spirit. Three in One.

This is a big concept to understand and even more difficult to explain. I am not going to take that on here. You can ask some fancy theologian type to explain it to you. All I know is that Jesus who came to Earth was the exact imprint of God. The Word became flesh and dwelt among us.

But when the fullness of time had come, God sent forth His Son, born of woman, born under the law to redeem those who were under the law, so that we might receive adoption as sons. (Galatians 4:4-5)

When the fullness of time had come, God sent His exact imprint to set us free. In God's perfect timing, He sent forth His perfect Son.

And when we accept a relationship through Jesus, we get the glorious gift of adoption as sons and daughters. Take a pause there for a Glory moment! You get the opportunity to be a child of God. An heir to the king. Our inheritance? Our inheritance is in heaven. We are simply making deposits for His kingdom while we are here on Earth.

God sent His exact imprint, and now we get to represent His imprint here on Earth.

It is no longer I who live, but Christ who lives in me. And the life I now live in the flesh I live by faith in the Son of God, who loved me and gave himself for me. (Galatians 4:20)

Sometimes, we just need the reminder that, as children of God, Christ lives in us.   Maybe you find your Christmas cheer turning to the Grinch as you are in the traffic around the mall this season. Or thinking about your extended family Christmas gathering makes you want to come down with a rare illness this year.

The life we live in our flesh is by faith in a God who loves us. All the time. He loves you so much that in the fullness of time, He came.

He. Came. For. You.

Christmas Heart Pause

Think about how the love of God has pursued you. Read Romans 8. The whole chapter. Let His deep love wash over your heart.

What sticks out to your heart most in reading Romans 8?

What area of your *fleshly feelings* can you take to the Lord in prayer, asking Him to show you ways Christ wants to live through you?

Day 13—The Halfway Point

There was a time when I was a runner. I just feel the strong need to tell you I ran a marathon once. I will admit, I try to bring that little fact into normal, everyday conversation as often as I can. I may run into you at the grocery store and you ask me if I happen to know where the cake mixes are. I will tell you that you can find the cake mixes on aisle two. Then, before you know it, I will slide marathon facts into the conversation. Two. That reminds me of the .2 in a marathon. 26.2 miles. That's the length of a run-until-you-think-you-are-going-to-die marathon. Did I mention I have run a marathon?

I am exaggerating of course, but I do proudly display my 26.2 miles sticker on my car just hoping that someone will ask me if I have run a marathon.

Why yes, I did in fact! Sure, by the time I finished running, the winner of the marathon had accepted his medal, flown home to his host country and had a banquet in his honor. Minor details. What matters is that I have the medal to prove that I finished that race (and that I never have to run or exercise again).

I remember that moment - the halfway point. Mile 13. The mile when I asked my sister, "Whose stupid idea was it to run a FULL marathon?" She kindly reminded me it was my "stupid idea." That mile marker was where I realized I was halfway there. Halfway through to the goal of the finish line. And that mile marker is where I wanted to quit. Give up. Stop. Turn around. Well, I did not really want to turn around. I wanted to lay down and have someone pick me up and magically transport me to the finish line. I was halfway there, and I was exhausted. I could not imagine going one more step.

Pushing through the "halfway point" is a decision we have to make. To keep going, to keep trying, to keep moving forward.

You are at the halfway point in this Christmas season. I am not sure how your Christmas season has been. Maybe it has been the most incredible season of your life. Or maybe it is the most difficult one you can remember. We all experience those "halfway" points in life where we want to lay down in exhaustion and stop fighting. The enemy of our soul will whisper, "Give up!"

He will whisper for you to stop fighting lies with the truth of God.

He will whisper all of the ways you are not enough, so you feel too exhausted to celebrate who you are because of Whose you are.

That sneaky Satan will try to keep you from continuing the race. He wants you stuck at the halfway point. He does not want you to come alive.

He is a liar and the father of lies. (John 8:44)

The thief comes only to steal and kill and destroy. I (Jesus) have come that they may have life and have it abundantly. (John 10:10)

Let's not give up at the halfway point.

Imagine if Mary and Joseph had given up halfway. What if Joseph decided halfway through Mary's pregnancy that it was too hard? What if he decided he did not want to follow the plan of God – that people's opinions and approval was more important than his obedience?

What if the wisemen had given up halfway through on their journey to find the baby Jesus. They would have missed the joy of laying their gifts at His feet.

We do get tired. We do get weary. The battle can get long, the spiritual warfare hard.

It can get hard to love people when they are proving to be un-loveable.

We realize halfway through living out a God-sized dream that there are things about our dream that are hard.

We can be following in obedience that which God has asked us to do and want to give up.

We can be thinking, "Whose idea was this anyway?"

Truth be told, I may be thinking that even in the writing of this devotional.

But God. But God promises He will grant us strength to follow through unless He is the one calling us to stop.

God granted Joseph the strength to not give up halfway.

God gave the wisemen a star to follow. God gave Mary a cousin named Elizabeth to confirm that which the angel had promised to her (Luke 1:39-45).

Jesus knew there would be times we would get tired, weary, and want to give up.

Come to me, all who labor and are heavy laden and I will give you rest. Take my yoke upon you, and learn from me, for I am gentle and lowly in heart and you will find rest for your souls. For my yoke is easy and my burden is light." (Matthew 11:28-29)

Are you at your halfway point? Come to Jesus, He promises rest. He will give you strength to continue, to not give up, strength to finish the race.

Christmas Heart Pause

What things in life are causing your heart to feel heavy laden? Place your name in Matthew 11:28-29.

Imagine wrapping those things that make you feel heavy and burdened as a Christmas gift. Picture wrapping each thing up and then laying these gifts at the feet of Jesus. It is a gift to Him for us to come to Him with our burdens. Then, He offers a divine gift exchange. He takes your burdens, and He gifts you with rest for your soul.

Rest my friend. Rest.

Day 14—Wonderful Counselor

These next few days, we are going to hang out in the names that are given to Jesus long before He was born. These lists of names were given by the prophet Isaiah. They were actually more descriptions then names. Names were very important in Old Testament days. You were named with a meaning.

For example, the story of the naming of Esau and Jacob, born to Isaac, Abraham's promised son. Esau, the firstborn of the twins, was named from the Hebrew word which meant "hairy". The exact description is found in Genesis 25:24. *"The first came out all red, all his body like a hairy clock, so they called his name Esau."* Wow. Red, hairy boy. Wonder if his friends made fun of him?

His twin brother came next. Jacob. He came out holding Esau's heel so they called him heel-grabber. Which also means "he cheats." Who wants to ask He Cheats to be on their baseball team? Jacob was aptly named, because He ended up cheating his hairy brother out of his birthright by offering him some tasty, red stew (Genesis 25:25-34).

For to us a child is born, to us a son is given; and the government shall be upon his shoulder, and his name shall be called Wonderful Counselor, Mighty God, Everlasting Father, Prince of Peace. (Isaiah 9:6)

I am glad that Jesus was not called by names that meant "hairy" or "he cheats." I feel that would make it a little bit harder to imagine the fulfillment of the promise that at the name of Jesus every knee will bow.

The first name in this list is Wonderful Counselor. I got my master's degree in Christian counseling, so I have a particular fondness for this description of Jesus.

Many times, I had clients assume that, along with the title "counselor," came my magic wand that I could wave and solve all their problems. As much as I wish I could find that wand, my wisdom is finite and limited. (Ps: Public Service Announcement that is probably to long for parenthesis. I am very "for" counseling. I think God uses human counselors in powerful ways. So please, do not think I am saying counseling is not a GREAT thing.)

When one goes to a counselor, you want to be heard. You want wisdom for the situation in which you find yourself.

I am so glad that Jesus came to the earth as a wonderful counselor so that we can be heard when we pray. Pre- Jesus days it was quite the ordeal to enter into the presence of God. You relied on the priests to take your offer before the Lord. Only one priest was really able to enter what they called the Holy of Holies.

Jesus made it possible for us to be heard by the God who created the heavens and the earth by prayer at any time, anywhere.

Let us then with confidence draw near to the throne of grace, that we may receive mercy and grace to help in time of need. (Hebrews 4:16)

Not only did the birth and death and resurrection of Jesus allow us to be heard by God, but God responds back to us.

Sometimes, it is hard to recognize the voice of God. We wish He would write the answer to our questions in the sky or on a sheet of paper.

God does still speak. He speaks through His word. Often, He will use others to speak to us. He also will use circumstances to speak.

I love this promise about our Wonderful Counselor.

If any of you lacks wisdom, let him ask God, who gives generously to all without reproach, and it will be given him. (James 1:5)

Our Wonderful Counselor is a generous wisdom-giver. I love that the word "generously" is in that verse.

Jesus promised us the Holy Spirit.

And I will ask the Father, and he will give you another Counselor, to be with you forever, even the Spirit of truth. (John 14:16-18)

Jesus may not be physically with you in your day, but the promised Holy Spirit is with us forever.

Christ in you, the hope of glory. (Colossians 1:27)

Christmas Heart Pause

In what circumstance today do you need wisdom? Praise God first, that He is a mighty counselor. Then, pray and ask for wisdom.

Read Isaiah 28:29. How have you seen God's wisdom displayed in your life?

Day 15—Mighty God

The next name in our Isaiah 9 description of Jesus is …. *Mighty God.*

Mighty.   A song I sang as a child comes to mind when I read the word mighty. (It even had hand motions).

My God is so big, so strong, and so mighty, there's nothing my God cannot do. (Repeat)

The mountains are his, the valleys are his, the stars are his handiwork too.

My God is so big, so strong, and so mighty, there's nothing my God cannot do.

For you.

We would always get excited and yell, "*For you!*" Our God is mighty to save—for you!

Our mighty God chose to come to earth as a meek baby. That baby Jesus knew He was the Messiah. He knew He would take the sins of the world in His nail pierced hands. Hands that flung the stars would be scarred—for our names to be written on His heart.

The mighty made meek. The meek still mighty.

That is the story of Christmas.

The other night I was tucking my favorite little man, my six year old nephew, into bed. He sat up straight and said, "Aunt Nenn, I need to ask you something!"

I had no idea where this would go, because he knows he can get anything he wants out of me. I assumed he would ask me if I could sneak him a donut or a sip of coffee or a scoop of ice cream. I have been known to do these things in the past with a wink and a grin.

He said, "Aunt Nenn, why do you not have a husband?" I was completely surprised by this question. I said, "Well, Alex, God has not brought Aunt Nenn a husband yet."

His eyes suddenly got very serious and he said, "Aunt Nenn, you need a husband. You need a husband to carry your heavy things!"

This made me laugh and laugh. I needed a husband simply to help me carry my heavy things.

It also made me pause. There was deep truth in that. We all need someone to carry our "heavy things." People are a blessing. So often, God will use His people to swoop in and minister right to our needs.

But ultimately, the only One who can carry my "heavy things" is the Holy One. The mighty God. The mighty God who made Himself fit in a manger.

Only the mighty God can carry the weight of our need for love. Only the mighty God truly has control of every situation.

I don't have an earthly husband, but I have a heavenly husband who can carry all of my "heavy things." Now, if you are a male reading this, I am sorry the husband analogy is probably much more difficult for you to wrap your heart around. But for a hopeless romantic, single girl—I just love that my Maker is my husband, and HE IS MIGHTY.

He is your mighty God. He is my mighty God.

The God who parted the Red Sea is your mighty God. The God who rescued Daniel from a lion's mouth—your mighty God. The God who had a whale swallow Jonah and then, in grace, spit him back out—your mighty God.

The Jesus who tore the veil between Heaven and Earth. He is your mighty God today. He was your mighty God yesterday. And He will be your mighty God tomorrow.

Our God is so BIG. So strong. And so mighty. There's nothing our God cannot do for you!

Christmas Heart Pause

Think of your favorite praise song that contains the word "mighty." (If you need some help, you can always use that glorious gift called Google.) Take a Christmas pause to praise our mighty God.

Read Psalms 24 about the mighty King of Glory.

What is a "heavy thing" you need for Him to carry?

Day 16—Everlasting Father

The next description in our power packed list of names for Jesus in Isaiah 9:6 is "Everlasting Father." I come to this descriptive name of God with a tender heart for you. I recognize that not everyone who is reading this had an earthly Father that represented our heavenly Father well. I want you to know that I am praying extra for you today. I am praying that, as you read the word Father, God wraps His arms tightly around your heart and whispers words of love and healing. I am also praying for the one who has lost your earthly Father. I am praying that, as you read these words, the Lord comforts your heart in the deepest places.

I was blessed with an incredible daddy. One who always had time to play, to listen, to hug, to protect. He spoke volumes to my little girl heart as a child when he resigned from a high position job because he did not have enough time to spend with us. He let his position go so we would know that we were a priority to him.

Wow. Our Everlasting heavenly Father did the same. He let His position in heaven go and came to Earth so that we would know that we are a priority to Him.

Have this mind among yourselves, which is yours in Christ Jesus, who though he was in the form of God, did not count equality with God a thing to be grasped, but made himself nothing, taking the form of a servant, being born in the likeness of men. And being found in human form, he humbled himself by becoming obedient to the point of death. (Philippians 2:5-8)

He made himself nothing to make sure you knew you were worth something. You were a priority to Him. You *are* a priority to Him.

I can think of many times my daddy showed me mercy, but one involving a "car incident" comes to my mind. I had been driving my sister's oh-so-cool white Corsica. She hated to drive, so I was usually the one who drove us around. I am not sure why she trusted me. I was driving us one time and may have gotten a smidge to close to someone's mailbox and knocked the side mirror off.

In all seriousness, I looked at my sister and said, "Wow, it's hot today. The glue just melted off the mirror."

She looked at me in all seriousness and said, "Jenn, you hit a mailbox!"

Well, here we were riding together again. Honestly, I am not sure what happened this time. I got distracted somehow. *I think I may have been thinking about a boy that I hoped to see at church that night.* Somehow, I hit a brick mailbox and a road sign. If only those silly mailboxes would stay out of my way. I damaged the car pretty badly – the quarter panel of the passenger side caved in badly.

You know that feeling of dread when you have to tell your parents you have done something bad. I woke my dad up when I got home that night and informed him that the car and I had "issues." I guess I was trying to blame the car for my hitting a huge brick mailbox and a road sign.

I do no really remember what happened next, but I know my daddy showed me grace. He was grateful that I was safe and home, and we would deal with the "car issues" in the morning.

Our heavenly Father is so patient with our "issues." He knows our hearts will bump into obstacles. That we will lose focus, get distracted, and wreck things at times. And He shows us grace.

Grace burst forth on this Earth.

She will bear a son, and you shall call his name Jesus, "for he will save his people from their sins." (Matthew 1:2)

This Christmas celebrate grace. Your heavenly Father is a gracious Dad.

For you did not receive the spirit of slavery to fall back into fear, but you have received the Spirit of adoption as sons, by whom we cry, "Abba! Father!" (Romans 8:15)

Christmas Heart Pause

Isaiah 9:6 calls Jesus "Everlasting Father." Think about the term "everlasting." What does that mean? Praise God for the fact that He is the same yesterday, today, and tomorrow.

Read James 1:17. Every good and perfect gift comes down from the Father of lights who does not change.

How does it feel to know that your everlasting Father does change?

Day 17—Prince of Peace

Peace. That word just makes you feel like you can pause and breathe. I extra-appreciate the idea of being able to breathe right now because I have one of those pesky colds where you cannot seem to use enough Kleenex, and you sound like you left some of the Kleenex stuffed up your nose.

By the way, in a running-out-of-Kleenex emergency, coffee filters work to. Just a random fact I feel like you should know.

The last descriptive name given to Jesus in Isaiah 9:6 is "Prince of Peace." The people hearing that prophecy were longing for peace. They were a nation constantly at war. Their story was a cycle of captivity and freedom and back to captivity again.

We also are a people longing for peace. Turn on the news, and your heart will long for peace. Walk through a crisis, and your heart will long for peace.

I find myself longing for peace when my people-pleasing-self feels I have been a failure.

I long for peace when I look at my bank account, or when my family is in crisis.

You may be longing for peace in your marriage, your home, your church.

You may be longing for peace when you think about trying to juggle all your school work and thinking, "Why did I decide to go to graduate school again?" You may be longing for peace about a decision you have to make. You may be longing to feel peace in your walk with Christ. You may be longing for peace in your household full of children.

Wherever you are longing for peace, the story of Christmas holds the promise of peace. The Prince of Peace.

I love fairy tales where a princess is rescued by a prince charming on a white horse. Actually, there does not even have to be a horse. Just a rescue and I like it.

Our Prince of Peace came to rescue us because He delighted in us. The angels singing about Jesus to the shepherds declared peace on earth.

Glory to God in the highest and on earth **peace** *among those with who is his pleased.* (Luke 2:14)

My pastor, Chris Jessen, preached a sermon on our thoughts this week that I am still chewing on. (You can find it at www.2rc.org on November 23rd.) Our spewing thoughts are often where our lack of peace starts.

What do you do when you get a phone call from your boss? Do you find your thoughts automatically going to *what have I done wrong this time?* When you get a phone call from your family member do you automatically starting going to all of the worst-case scenarios?

Are your thoughts a place of peace or a place of chaos?

You keep him in perfect peace whose mind is stayed on you, because he trusts in you. (Isaiah 26:3)

Come alive this Christmas by refocusing your thoughts on the Prince of Peace. The truth that Jesus had a promised plan to come and rescue you, and He fulfilled His promises.

The wisemen found Jesus because they stayed focused on following the star.

We can find Jesus by staying focused on the star of Christmas, Jesus Himself. And Jesus is the Prince of Peace.

Peace I leave with you. Not as the world gives do I give to you. Let not your hearts be troubled, neither let them be afraid. (John 14:27)

"Peace I leave with you." Receive those words as a gift today.

Christmas Heart Pause

Peace. What does that word mean to you? When is a time you have experienced peace.

Read Philippians 4:7-9. What do these verses have to say about peace?

Pause for a moment and let the peace of God wash over you.

Day 18—Following the Star

We all have dreams and callings of some sort. They may look different for each one of us, but God has planted a dream and a calling to fulfill in you and through you.

For we are his workmanship, created in Christ Jesus for good works, which God prepared beforehand, that we should walk in them. (Ephesians 2:10)

How do you take the steps towards the dream, the steps of obedience to answer the calling God has for you?

The key is you start, you keep your focus, and you follow the One who planted those dreams.

We had a little Christmas tragedy a few years ago. We had a star topper on top of our Christmas tree that had been there for years and years. It had even survived the years of the "Handy Twins" do-it-yourself show. We have had to rig it over the years. In fact, the base of the star had become a glue stick holder that my dad had fixed up.

This year's conversation went something like this. "I need the duct tape, a binder clip, scissors, glue, and another glue stick holder to fix this bad boy to go up on top of the tree."

My mom's practical response was, "Mike, it's probably time to get another star for the tree if you have to have that many supplies to fix the star."

The whole thing makes me laugh. But it also makes me think about another star.

Matthew 2 tells the story of wise men from the east finding Jesus. They were having a hard time locating Him, even going to the wrong person to find out where he may be. They stopped by the palace of Herod and asked Him for directions. Sneaky Herod acted like he also wanted to find where Jesus was to throw Him a big, royal baby shower. Reality was, he wanted to kill Him. Praise the Lord an angel warned the wise men in a dream, and they did not send a message back to Herod when they found Jesus.

They found Jesus because they saw the star in the East. They followed it to find Him and worship Him.

They kept their gaze on that star to find the One to worship. They followed it. I am sure at times they wondered where they were going. I imagine they got tired on their journey.

Maybe, at times, their camels did not cooperate.

Maybe they wondered how they would find food.

Maybe they felt crazy at times. Maybe they wondered what others would think.

But they followed it. They followed the star because they were focused on worshipping the Messiah, the Savior, Christ the Lord.

They took the first steps. Then the next steps. Then the next.

They kept their focus, and they found their Savior, and gave Him their gifts.

That's what following God in obedience should be. Taking my first step, then the next, then the next. Even when, at times, I wonder where I am going. Or when I get tired. Or when things do not go as planned.

Following for the purpose of worshipping the King of glory.

Christmas Heart Pause

Read the story of the wise men in Matthew 2.

Think about your own journey. What detours have you experienced? How has keeping your eyes on the Savior kept you walking in obedience?

What steps of obedience is God directing you toward? What gifts can you lay before the King?

Day 19—The Cry of the Cross

Have you ever been in the room when a new baby is born? True confession, I have not, but I have watched movies. Once a baby is born, it seems everything in the room becomes still as you wait for that newborn baby to take his or her first breath. You know the baby has taken its first breath when it lets out a good old-fashioned cry.

Just stop and imagine with me the scene in heaven the day Jesus was born. I imagine that heaven was still for a moment—quiet with a collective holding of the heavenly breath as all the angels waited for God-made-flesh to take His first breath.

Imagine the moment when Jesus made that first cry. In that cry, all of heaven knew there would be a cross.

The King of Kings came to Earth as a baby with a plan of redemption in mind.

The minute He first cried, Jesus knew He would one day utter a loud cry on the cross. This loud cry on the cross would cause the heavens to stop and the earth to shake.

With his hands and feet nailed to a cross made of wood, He cried out these powerful words.

…and Jesus said, "Father, forgive them, for they know not what they do." (Luke 2:34)

Later, He cried these other words from the cross.

When Jesus had received the sour wine, he said, "It is finished," and he bowed his head and gave up his spirit. (John 19:30)

The first cry of baby Jesus offered us the gift of the cry of the cross.

The finished work of our Savior led to the forgiveness of our sins and the salvation of our souls.

The resurrection story is not just to be celebrated at Easter. The resurrection story started with the birth of our Savior.

The story does not end with the innocence of a little baby. It does not end as the innocent one—the sinless one Jesus, takes our sins upon himself on the cross.

The story ends on that someday when He is coming back to rule and reign, no longer a crying baby or a man crucified on a cross, but as King.

Christmas Heart Pause

Read the "end of the story" in Revelation 21 and 22.

Day 20—O Christmas Tree

In case you have not figured me out by now, I am a cheesy Christmas girl. I love a good Hallmark movie marathon, while wearing comfy Christmas pajamas, of course.

My sister's and my favorite Christmas music for years (besides the spiritual stuff of course) has been the Alabama Christmas CD. We would blast "Thistle Hair the Christmas Bear" as loud as we could on repeat. I am not so sure my fellow dorm mates in college appreciated that.

My family's Christmas tree has an ornament on it from every year since my parents were married in 1979. We love to put all those ornaments on the tree and remember what the story of that year was. You can tell some of the years were more "lean" than others. There is the ornament from the year we visited Disneyworld. Or the Hallmark ornament angel that lights up. Or, my favorite, the one from the year my sister and I were conceived that says, "Christmas is for merry making." (Insert sheepish grin here.)

My Christmas tree is not as large and full as my parents. In fact, it has to be taped to the wall to stand up straight! However, this tree does have some fun memories.

I have collected some crazy ornaments. My precious Thursday night Bible study ladies and I do a crazy ornament exchange every year. These always make me smile when I think of who gave them to me. Like the giant green sparkly mushroom from my friend Kathy. It totally fits her sparkling personality.

I have a yak from Nepal, a coffee cup from a London Starbucks, and a handmade village woman from Bangladesh.

Every year the tree looks a little different because I keep adding on.

I remember one particular moment when I was looking at my Christmas tree a few years ago. It had been a very difficult year. In November of that year, while I was visiting Nepal, I had to quickly return home when the doctors found my dad had a rare form of aggressive bladder cancer. I had watched him go through a very difficult surgery and a long road of recovery. That Christmas, my roommate and best friend was getting married, and I knew I would begin living alone. I was so happy for her, but sad for the changes it was bringing.

I had cried myself to sleep that night, and then I walked into my living room. The living room with the shag carpet 1970's throwback. I saw the Christmas tree full of memories. And the Lord spoke to my heart.

Jenn, I do not change. I am the light of your world. I am the one who causes your life to sparkle and shine.

I am the one building memories with you all year long.

I love the crazy things about you—in fact I created you.

I will never leave you. Even though the year may bring change, I do not change.

We will keep making memories.

So, I wanted to remind you (and me) as we come alive this Christmas. The Lord does not change. He has prepared the most fun memories for us to make together. Like a Christmas tree has memories from many years, our heart is a tree to display His glory.

Through each circumstance, the good and the bad, he is hanging ornaments on the branches of my heart.

These ornaments of His glory point upward, sparkling and reflecting His light.

I pray the Christmas tree of my heart looks beautiful to Him and stands as a memorial to the good memories we are making together.

Christmas Heart Pause

What are your favorite ornaments on your tree? What do these memories represent?

What are your favorite memories with Jesus this year?

Read Hebrews 13:8 and celebrate that Jesus is the same even when things change.

Make some sort of ornament to represent the way you have experienced Jesus this year.

Day 21—Surprises from the Lord

Christmas is generally a time spent with family. If you do not have family close by this Christmas, I am going to pray you find a family to adopt yourself into. I would welcome you to the Hand family Christmas, but I am just warning you, you never know what will happen.

A story that is often overlooked in our telling of the Christmas story is that of a relative of Jesus, John the Baptist. He was born around the same time as Jesus. John the Baptist was born with his purpose to be the one who prepared the way for Jesus. We would later find John the Baptist in his simple missionary clothes doing what missionaries do—eating bugs and proclaiming about Jesus. Ok, the truth is, I think I have heard that the locusts John the Baptist ate were really a type of leaf from a tree, and not all missionaries eat bugs. But, when you are a missionary, you may have to eat bugs, so I think this is a fun way to look at. I never had to eat a bug as a missionary, but I did have to eat a live fish once.

They rolled that tank over to my table, and I thought it was our personal aquarium for scenery while we ate. No, it was full of what we were going to eat! I will never forget them handing me that live goldfish and me swallowing it— and it swimming all the way down. That same meal a live slug was placed on a tea candle to do a dance. It danced on my chopstick as I ate it.

I digress.

John the Baptist was born to Zechariah and Elizabeth. They were the New Testament version of Abraham and Sarah. They were card carrying members of the AARP and had no children.

They had not received the desire of their heart for children, but they were faithful. God is always working out a plan, even when we do not see His answers. What a powerful compliment of faithfulness was said of Zechariah and Elizabeth. They had not received the answer they were looking for, but Luke 1:6 describes their relentless faithfulness.

...and they were both righteous before God, walking blamelessly in all of the commandments and statutes of the Lord."

And then came the surprise. Zechariah was serving as priest. Getting ready to do his normal, priestly duties.

Often, it is when we are going about our normal, everyday routine God shows up to remind us He is able to do the extraordinary.

An angel appeared on the right side of the altar of incense. Then the angel said the thing angels apparently tended to say, *"Do not be afraid."* If you notice the pattern, when an angel shows up and tells you that, he is probably going to give you a big surprise announcement from the Lord.

The angel then tells Zechariah that his wife Elizabeth was going to bear a son. It's easy to point our spiritual finger, but I imagine I may have said the same thing Zechariah said. *"How can this be?"*

The angel sentenced him to silence for that question.

I am grateful the Lord has not sentenced me to silence every time I ask the question, *"How can this be."* I lost my voice for a long time while in college and had to write everything on a dry erase board. I went through a fortune's worth of dry erase markers.

The Lord surprised Zechariah and Elizabeth with a fulfillment of a long-prayed-for desire. Do not give up praying my friend. God will answer. Always.

It may not be in the time you expect.

Or the plan expect.

Or the place expect.

But, be on the lookout because our God is a God full of surprises!

Christmas Heart Pause

When was the last time you received a surprise from the Lord?

Read the story of Hannah's surprise in 1 Samuel 1 and 2. When the Lord surprises you with His answers, are you willing to give the answer back to Him?

Day 22—Childlike Wonder

Children get so excited at Christmas. They do not worry about how much things cost, about trying to get everything done, or about trying to get the perfect picture for the family Christmas card.

Children get excited with a simple wonder.

I pray that, as you come alive at Christmas, you can experience childlike wonder.

Last night, I got the best call from my precious nephew, Alex. He said, "Aunt Nenn, I believe in Jesus. I prayed to accept Christ and asked Him for a clean heart."

He was filled with such childlike wonder.

My sister said he was going around sharing the plan of salvation to his 2 year old and 4 month old sisters because he wanted them to have the same excitement that he had.

He was filled with such childlike wonder.

I want to be filled with childlike wonder.

I also want to be filled with Mary-like wonder. After Mary visited her cousin Elizabeth, she spoke this beautiful word of praise in Luke 1:46-56. My Bible calls it the Magnificat.

I am going to put your Christmas heart pause right here in the middle of this day. Would you read this with me with Mary-like wonder? You have been told that you are pregnant with the son of God, that the baby inside of you has been conceived by the Holy Spirit.

You have been visited by an angel. You have visited your relative, who confirmed what the angel had promised you. You are overwhelmed by a mixture of fear and excitement—literally pregnant with anticipation about what the Lord has planned for you.

Mary-like wonder.

…and Mary said, "My soul magnifies the Lord, and my spirit rejoices in God my Savior, for he has looked on the humble estate of his servant. For behold, from now on all generations will call me blessed; for he who is mighty has done great things for me, and holy is his name. And his mercy is for those who fear him from generation to generation. He has shown strength with his arm, he had scattered the proud in the thoughts of their hearts, he has brought down the mighty from their thrones and exalted those of humble estate; he has filled the hungry with good things, and the rich he has sent away. (Luke 1:46-54)

Now think about what work the Lord is doing in your life. Has done in your life. Would you take a Christmas pause and write your own Magnificat, filled with Mary-like wonder?

Day 23—Jesus Presented at the Temple

Baby dedication day is always a beautiful day at a church. Anything with a cute squishy-cheeked baby is special to watch. Add the joy in the parents' eyes as they hold their child before the church, and it is a very sweet and sacred moment to watch. There is also that fear you can sense as the parents pray their child does not scream, cry, or make a scene while being dedicated to the Lord.

I was unable to be at my niece's recent baby dedication service, but I saw the video of it. My dad captured the moment in perfect timing. The moment where something besides "the Spirit" moved in my tiny little 3 month old niece. Let's just say, in the middle of my pastor praying, there was a major explosion!

I imagine you can picture the expression on my sister's face. In case you cannot, I will describe it to you. Sterling (the pastor) was praying over baby Abigail, and Michelle notices something in the hand which is holding Abbi. The look on her face is Candid Camera-worthy. The I–don't-know-what-to-do-now, I wish-he-would-stop-praying moment. That special gift began to run all over my sister and her dress. My mom and her mother-in-law were giving her the D*o you know what is happening?* look from the crowd.

I do not think my sister will ever forget that moment where they prayed for Abigail to be set apart for the Lord.

Luke 2:22 tells the story of Jesus being presented at the temple. The time had come for Joseph and Mary to take Jesus to be presented to the Lord in the temple. I am sure they are more spiritual than I would be.

If it were me, I think when they were lining up the children to be dedicated, I would be sure to let everyone know – this is not your ordinary baby, friends. This is – well—the Son of God. We are His earthly parents. Would you like our signed *How to Raise the Son of God* memoir now or later?

I am sure Mary and Joseph did not act this way.

There was a man in Jerusalem named Simeon. This man was filled with the Holy Spirt. He was described as a righteous and devout man.

Simeon lived in the prayerful expectancy of help for Israel. (Luke 1:25, MSG)

He spent his days worshipping and waiting. As he worshipped and waited, the Holy Spirit revealed to him that he would not see death before he saw the Lord Jesus Christ.

So He continued to worship and wait.

Have you noticed there is a great deal of waiting in the stories of Christmas? The anticipation for years of a promised Messiah. The nine months of waiting for Mary. The years of waiting for Simeon.

Watching and waiting. Worshipping in the waiting.

When Simeon saw Jesus in the temple that day, he instantly knew. He knew he was meeting the one he had been waiting for.

I just recently held the hand of my precious grandfather as he took his last earthly breath and met Jesus in heaven. It had been days of watching him intensely suffer. But the moment when he met Jesus was such a hard holy. Hard for us, because we had to say goodbye. Holy because waiting for someone to meet Jesus is indeed Holy Ground.

His beautiful blue eyes opened right before he took his last breath, and I knew—I knew he had seen. He had seen what his heart had been waiting for. The King of Kings, the Lord of Lords, revealed in all His glory, taking him home.

The wait was over.

...he took him up in his arms and blessed God and said, " Lord, now you are letting your servant depart in peace, according to your word; for my eyes have seen your salvation that you have prepared in the presence of all peoples, a light for revelation to the Gentiles, and for glory to your people Israel." (Luke 2:28-32)

His eyes had seen what he was looking for. His Savior.

What are your eyes looking for this Christmas?

Christmas Heart Pause

What is your heart looking for?

Read the story of Ann the prophetess in Luke 2:36-38. This is the story of another who was watching and worshipping.

What is one way you have learned to worship while you wait?

Day 24—We Lost Jesus

Have you ever found yourself lost in a crowd? Worse yet, have you ever lost someone in a crowd?

If you have lost someone, you know that gut-wrenching, stomach-dropping feeling that comes when you realize the person that you thought was beside you is gone. Lost in a sea of faces.

You search frantically for them. Calling their name. Running. Asking other people to help you find the one that you have lost.

Imagine the crowded streets at a parade. That was the scene when Jesus's parents went to Jerusalem at the Feast of Passover. Jesus was 12 years old, and it was time for them to take the customary trip to those crowded streets. The feast was over, and it was time for them to return home.

They started the journey home on those crowded streets. Mary was probably chatting it up with all the other mothers of teenage boys. Joseph was talking with other carpenters about their trade. They traveled for a whole day, and it came time for them to set up camp for the night. Mary called to Jesus and could not seem to find him. Maybe she was calm at first, as she began to search for Him among their relatives and friends.

Then panic set in. Jesus was nowhere to be found.

Can you imagine the mommy guilt that must have settled in her heart? *I just lost the Son of God.* Wow. How do you explain that one? Emmanuel, God with us—He's, well, he's no longer with us. Have you seen him?

They returned back to Jerusalem, retracing their steps, hoping to find Him.

And they did. **After three days.** Can you imagine— three days. They were worried; Jesus was not.

They found Him sitting in the temple, among the teachers, listening, and asking questions.

And all who heard him were amazed at his understand and his answers. And when His parents saw him, they were astonished. (Luke 2:47-48)

Mary did what any other mama would do, "*Son why have you treated us so?*" Translation. If you were not the son of God, you would be in SO much trouble. You gave me and your Father a heart attack!

…and he said to them, "Why were you looking for me? Did you not know that I must be in my Father's house?" (v. 49)

Friends, it can be so easy for us to "lose Jesus". We get busy on our journeys. We have our to-do lists to accomplish. Our friends to see. Our church work to do.

We have our family to take care of. Our bills to pay, our kids to take to soccer practice.

We have a piano recital to go to, a Christmas cookie making party, a pan full of sausage balls to make—and we volunteered to take turkeys to the homeless.

We have to please and perform.

None of these things are bad. Many of them are good things.

But, let's make sure we do not lose Jesus. I do not want to lose Jesus on the road to my everyday life.

I don't want to leave church on Sunday and return home and not realize I have lost him until three days later at prayer meeting on Wednesday.

I do not want to lose Jesus in the crowd. I want to come alive with Jesus, hanging out with Him in His Father's house.

Christmas Heart Pause

Read the story of Jesus in the temple in Luke 2:41-52.

Verse 52 speaks of Jesus increasing in wisdom and stature and favor with God. Ask God for this to be your story as you come alive at Christmas. Ask Him to help you grow in wisdom and favor with God.

Where in your life do you think you have lost Jesus?

Day 25—It's Christmas Day

I get to this day with mixed emotions. Taking this Coming Alive at Christmas journey with you has been an incredible gift to me. The Lord has spoken such new deep truths to my heart, making Christmas come alive in a new way to me. I pray the same for you.

I pray, as you open gifts today, that your heart has been opened in whole new ways to the gift of Christmas.

Emmanuel. God with us.

A Savior, which is Christ the Lord. A savior who knew what He was going to sacrifice. Himself.

The steadfast love of the Lord never ceases, his mercies never come to an end; they are new every morning, great is your faithfulness. (Lamentations 3:22-23)

I've always felt a little let down after Christmas morning. I knew that, soon, the last Christmas cookie would be eaten, the Christmas songs would end, that the Christmas tree would have to be packed back in the attic. This is my LEAST favorite job-- which is why my Christmas tree stayed out until February last year. And I do not have an attic. So I did not even know where to pack the Christmas tree!

The excitement of Christmas morning fades. The gifts are unwrapped. The family goes home. Another Christmas is done.

When celebrating the Jesus of Christmas, there is no let down. The gift of the love of the Lord never ceases. His mercies are new **every morning.** Every minute. We can unwrap the gift of Christmas anytime, anywhere.

Emmanuel came so that we could live the *with God* life. God with us.

She will bear a son, and you shall call his name Jesus, for he will save his people from their sins. All this took place to fulfill what the Lord had spoken by the prophet: "Behold the virgin shall conceive and bear a son, and they shall call his name Immanuel," (which means God with us). When Joseph woke from sleep, he did as the angel of the Lord commanded him; he took his wife but knew her not until she had given birth to a son. And he called his name Jesus. (Matthew 1:21-25)

Jesus. Not to be cliché, but He really is the greatest gift. In Jesus, we get to unwrap forgiveness, peace, love, joy, strength, power, and the gift of eternity.

Eternity will be one, big Christmas morning (and will maybe even include footie pajamas)!

Christmas Heart Pause

What new gifts have you unwrapped as you have come alive this Christmas?

What do you sense Jesus asking you to do with these gifts?

Lord I pray for my friends who have taken this 25 days to Coming Alive at Christmas heart challenge. Lord I pray for all of us, that You renew our hearts and our minds with the truth found in the miracles of Christmas. Thank You that we were on Your mind, even in the manger. That You knew the cradle would lead to the cross. And You chose, in love, to come. You chose to leave the halls of heaven to walk the streets of Earth. You love us with an indescribable love. I pray for my friends—that they will begin to understand how high, long, wide and deep is Your love for them. That You have called them by name. That they are Yours. That they will worship as they wait, and when we lose You Jesus—that we will look for You in Your Father's house.

About Jenn

Jenn is a coffee loving (well maybe obsessed) Jesus girl. She accepted Christ's invitation to come alive at eight years old and has been so blessed by His love ever since. She is known to go to the playground and swing, go all over the world without a map or a plan and spoil her nephew and nieces rotten.

Jenn has a Master's degree in professional counseling with an emphasis on spiritual direction. If Jenn could, she would ask you to have a cup of coffee with her and she would ask you what makes you come alive. Jenn is the executive director/keynote speaker for Coming Alive Ministries and is having a blast living her God sized dream.

In 2014 her first book *31 days to Coming Alive* was published, reaching the Amazon Bestsellers List.

Jenn would love to connect with you at:

- Website at comingaliveministries.com
- Facebook at facebook.com/comingaliveministries
- Instagram and Twitter as @comingalivejenn

If you are looking for a conference or retreat speaker, Jenn would love to connect with you. E-mail comingaliveministries@gmail.com for more information.

About Coming Alive Ministries

Coming Alive Ministries, a 501 (c)3 registered non-profit, was founded in May 2012 to provide an invitation to come alive in Christ through conferences, Christian life coaching, and written resources.

Since 2012, Coming Alive has done over 50 retreats nationally and internationally. We would love for you to join us at one of our Bloom Conferences throughout the year. These conferences are designed for ladies age 12-122 to come away for the weekend and connect with Christ through a time of fellowship, worship, and the Word. We also would love to bring the "conference in a box" Bloom style to you!

Connect with us at www.comingaliveministries.com

.

Made in the USA
Middletown, DE
04 December 2015